I0151427

BLACK EYE

poems by

Sharon Dennis Wyeth

Finishing Line Press
Georgetown, Kentucky

BLACK EYE

Copyright © 2018 by Sharon Dennis Wyeth
ISBN 978-1-63534-463-9 First Edition
All rights reserved under International and Pan-American Copyright Conventions.
No part of this book may be reproduced in any manner whatsoever without written
permission from the publisher, except in the case of brief quotations embodied in
critical articles and reviews.

ACKNOWLEDGEMENTS

The poet acknowledges with thanks previous publication of the following
poems:

"Mother's Back" (*Drunken Boat*, Volume 8),
"Weather" (*Cave Canem* Anthology XI),
"Dog Dream 2: (*The Hollins Critic*),
"Her Blood" (*Cave Canem* Anthology XII),
"*sug*" (*Hollins Critic*),
"Tikar Reuion" (*Cura* Magazine),
"Hibiscus" (*10x10, Cave Canem*)

Publisher: Leah Maines
Editor: Christen Kincaid
Cover Art: Sharon Dennis Wyeth family photo
Author Photo: Phil Cantor
Cover Design: Elizabeth Maines McCleavy

Printed in the USA on acid-free paper.
Order online: www.finishinglinepress.com
also available on amazon.com

Author inquiries and mail orders:
Finishing Line Press
P. O. Box 1626
Georgetown, Kentucky 40324
U. S. A.

Table of Contents

Age Three: in the Quiet..1

The Closet..2

Mother's Back..3

In a white enveloped marked
Do not open until my death:..4

Caption: *Black eye*..5

Ghost Gossip..6

Dog Dream 1..10

Remarkable..11

Weather..12

"Cracker"..13

Dog Dream 2..17

Scribe..18

Buttons..19

Premonition..20

Tale..21

They..22

Poison..23

Behind a Blue Door..24

Her Blood..25

The Sin of It..26

Chain..27

Raindrops..28

"*sug*"..29

Tikar Reunion..30

Dog Dream 3..31

Hibiscus..32

for Evon, Always

Age Three: in the Quiet

I was sitting on the couch
I heard you coming from
the bedroom in the back

You stopped in the hallway,
opened the door to the bathroom
I heard it shut
Then it opened up again

You stepped into the living room
holding something gray and limp
taken from the trap

You held it in my face,
called me scaredy-cat
and swung the broken creature by its tail

The Closet

We are in the closet,
my mommy and me

I was crying so
my daddy let me in

There is no seeing
in this darkness

but she reaches out for me
Her arms are clammy

She says: "Please…let us out
"Let out the child at least"

Mother's Back

My mother's back
in navy blue
in winter white
in sleeveless gray

slips down the stairs
into the night
to flee his wrath
But she comes back

We escape
in rubber boots
My mittens bleed
on her pale coat

Mother's back,
powder puffed,
sheathed in silver,
splashed with roses,

trotting out for fun at last
My mother's back,
not quite broken

In a white envelope marked
Do not open until my death:

> A letter
> two postcards
> (remarkably preserved)
> and a square inch picture
> taken in a photo-mat,
> bound in soft tin frame,
> captioned top left:

> *Black eye*

> Here they lie:
> my mother's ruined face,
> my father's letter of remorse,
> postcards he sent me after he left

Caption: *Black eye*

I was there,
not in the photo,
not in the photo-mat,
but on the planet
Just old enough to recall
when she was thrown
against the wall

Here are the facts:
The woman in the picture
is 21 years and five months old
In the one inch square black and white,
the kind you pay for in a booth,
the coat she wears is blue
Above the blackened eye
is a lock of long brown hair
Staring straight ahead,
she is plotting her next move

Ghost Gossip

All I wanted was a gossip bench
and for that girl to tell her mother
I hadn't called her an EFF-ing banana.
Didn't even know that word, *fuN-king*
banana is what I called outside her window,
not being mean, being funny,
but nobody believed me,
so Mother scrubbed my tongue with soap
and my friend's mother said
I couldn't play with her again.

Wanted my boyfriend at the door,
my father letting him in
so they could talk electronics.
My boyfriend whose first name
was the same as my last name
and who wanted to be the same thing
as my daddy when he grew up.

But that was before I met *him*
the new one from Tuskegee,
who fooled me with his wings
and blinded me with his skin
so white I couldn't see
when he pulled down my panties.
Choked by his beauty,
I forgot about the rubber
like Mother had warned me
since the day I got my period
if the time should come
 I should say:
Not without a rubber, buddy!

If my old boyfriend had knocked
on the door right that minute,
I might have been saved
from the one with wings who beat me
and I married in a hurry
even though I still weighed ninety
and hadn't felt a thing
except the hurt that came
because he couldn't fit.

Wanted most of all
that Daddy kick his ass
instead of calling him son
because his skin was light
and yet he didn't pass and wore those wings
to prove he was a gifted colored man;
buttering Daddy up, calling him "*Doc.*"
Can you blame me for shopping on the sly?

It was Easter and my boys needed caps
but then I left the shopping bag on the bus.
Thank the lord, I didn't lose the white bolero
I picked up on sale—hid that in the hallway.
I had to cover my shoulders with something,
didn't I? since the dress was more for evening
than for a Confirmation on the day
when I would turn Episcopalian?
 Might as well have had my shoulders bare,
he was jealous of the preacher, so he beat me.

I thought, if I just had me a gossip bench
to sit down with the phone and call my friend
to tell her all about it, even though she was his cousin
and the one who introduced us, she would make him stop
or maybe not.

There was that time with his sisters
on the brand new sectional sofa,
my little girl sitting with them,
him and his brother in the kitchen
sipping Tru-Aide with their gin
and I come in wearing my hostess pajamas,
straight from Japan, black silk pants and orange top,
to get dragged back to the bedroom
to be punched for parading half undressed.
His brother and his sisters didn't notice
I was screaming or the handkerchiefs
with the lipstick I had plastered on the wall?

All I wanted was my little girl
not to be treated like that by any man
even if he's colored with white skin
or by the white men either when you're pregnant,
standing on the bus and dizzy with diabetes,
holding back your tears not to throw up
and they stand to give their seat
to a woman who is white and just got on.

All I wanted was for the maid of honor gown
not to be burned with the butt of a cigarette
before my sister's wedding when the man
I married stopped by at the church.
And for my kids to have a school
without the paint chips and some books.

All because I spread my legs.
If I had not done that one thing,
I would have been someone else
instead of married to a man who couldn't sing,
and liked the numbers, who had never seen a play
and crossed the line to fake it at the office
which I found it hard to stomach,
even though I liked the money.

All I wanted was to not wake up at 3 a.m.
to make a tomato and mayonnaise sandwich
with sliced onion and watch him throw it up.

Just wanted not to be scared all the time,
with four children and a job at twenty-three.
I was supposed to be playing Paderewski
in a school in Boston, my mother's daughter
in a gingham dress with blue buttons
and the ring Daddy gave me with my birthstone
and the watch from my auntie in Chicago
who's a real live PhD.
Let me go back to West Virginia
where my sister brushed my hair
a hundred times across the bed.

Only I would still want the kids,
just with a man who didn't hit
and who had a picket fence and a Cadillac
with all the fixings and affairs
we would attend with his club
and the lunches I'd make for mine,
in a house with a sectional sofa
and a panther on the mantle and china
with red flowers and gold trim
and silver plate we would keep in a chest,
and I'd be pretty without a neck brace
or black eye and he'd be handsome with brown skin.
But that was not to be. *Honey lamb—*
I got out of there. Left that gossip bench behind.

Dog Dream 1

Black dog choking
I squeeze her bloated belly
She coughs up rubber ball,
green plastic alligator
Breathe

Sweet dog wheezing
My hair upon her fur
Throat burned acid,
choked on childhood
Breathe

Remarkable

Dear Dad,
When your fist fell into Mom's face, I fell into a crater
Now I find your letter, forty years later

> *You told me once that if I left town*
> *it would solve your problems. After New Year's*
> *Eve when you tried to have me arrested, said*
> *I would be in jail on Tuesday morning I decided*
> *that was best.*

Best forget you
I decided when you left

> *Know you are hard pressed*
> *for money. I will try and have all seventy*
> *by the First, though nothing can be done...*

We found coins inside the couch,
ate spam for Sunday dinner,
taped our shoes to keep the soles from flapping

> *I went to a Catholic church to-night the service was*
> *quite   remarkable   beautiful church on 8th Ave &*
> *34th St in the heart of Manhattan.*

I know the place, dropped by when I turned thirty
Sought a priest, got advice,
kept on living

You write
        I am sorry.
I'm sorry, too,
for the long delay
Your letter wasn't mailed to me—
        "remarkable"
 no more to say

Weather

It was a bright day
the first time I walked by myself to school
up the mighty hill, one of the crowd,
ears catching laughter, feet Buster Brown,
floating on a lazy wave of sunbeams

Then a cloud came,
a pair of gray pants with no face,
a burn in my middle

I don't know if he led me away
or if it happened on the street,
but when I kept on walking,
my shiny shoes were muddy
and I wondered how I got to be alone

Two teachers stood in the open doorway
Words formed in my mind, something
my mother told me I needed to say
if ever it should happen—
                "someone touched me."

"This child says someone touched her."
On the brightest of days

"Cracker"

Outside our place on Vernon Street,
skinny butt leaning against a two-tone Chevy,
flat chest in one of them halters,
my back feeling the burn of the metal,
I'm standing with a boy, when he asks:
      "You a *cracker*?"
I see a bowl of chicken noodle soup
with floating saltines: "no-*oo*"
Daddy and Uncle Frank on the stoop
They'd pushed the Chevy up the hill
on account of a broke down battery
      "That your Daddy?"
"Yes"—Daddy—pink shirt, sunglasses—
      "The *white* man?"
Daddy's pink sleeve rolled up, his arm—
Uncle Frank's with yellow sleeve was—
brown—I had not noticed.
In the dark, the night before
the boy and I had played
draw a magic circle on an ol' man's back
He'd traced a spot between my shoulders
but today:
      "You just like your daddy, girl.
      You a *cracker* too."

Inside the apartment, stomach pressed
against the edge of the table, fingertips placed
on the shiny gray trim, I watch my mother
wield a butcher knife above a head of pale green cabbage
"What's a *cracker*?"
The knife slashes through, brown eyes flicker
"Where'd you hear that?"
"A boy."
 Long dark hair falls in a wave to graze the slaw
"You know what a cracker is, angel, something you eat with soup."

Wrong—I know that on account of the needle in my chest
"Go outside and play, or if that boy's still there,
look at tv. Pinky Lee's on—hungry?"
"Got a *cracker*?" I say slyly
"No crackers, here. How about a cookie?"

Wolfing down Oreos, the needle wiggles through me
I hop on one foot, laugh when I'm not supposed to,
say *mirror, mirror on the wall* in my mind,
skipping the *fairest* part, which don't make no sense
because it has too many meanings—fairest as in that ain't right?
or as in pretty Snow White? or like them cousins on Mommy's side
who Daddy doesn't know but they're just as blonde and blue eyed
as his people are and *fair* like Mommy's daddy—
my Granddaddy who is a no-color, not a crayon-color anyway
or cracker-floating-in-the-soup color—
but Mommy says she has the proof that her father was blonde
in that picture when he was a boy holding his teddy bear—
she just has to find it—'cause that's why my hair's blonde,
'cause I take after her side too, even though in the manger
at Vacation Bible School, blonde is straw and my hair is not
Not a cracker, either, but try telling someone else that

On the way from school when we move to Anacostia,
boys with rocks hide behind telephone poles
Sudden stinging hurt on my calf
Stumbling, holding tight to little brother's hand
Rocks keep coming—"Crackers!"
"Leave me and my brother alone!"
Day after day running past the precinct, then the bakery,
through the doughnuts smells we cannot stop to sniff,
we make it to the corner where the crossing guard stands waiting
Little brother bats back tears—"are we *crackers*?"
Stop to breathe— "no, we're Negroes."

One night for supper, oyster stew,
little brother will not eat, while I tell
"Keep on walkin'," Mommy murmurs.
Daddy yells "Hell no, you hit back!"
So I beat up a boy with my Christmas umbrella
'til all the spokes are broke—he jumped me, see,
coming home with my rock collection;
precious found-stones flying out of the shoe box,
the box top with their names written in cursive
sandstone, granite, stomped by his boot
I'd gotten an A and my mother hadn't seen it
Don't care he's on the ground, crying
Don't care where I aim, leave him crumpled
No one calls me cracker after that

In Nana's back alley the winter I'm nine,
I see the real thing
Three of 'em come tippin' up,
white tennis shoes, no socks or coats
Three little ghosts "Who're they?"
—my insides quivering—
        "Crackers," that from my friend Cyn
who jumps rope with me and loves buttered toast
 She picks up a rock and starts to chase
their so pale legs beneath the cotton dresses,
their string hair flying—
"white cracker chew tobacco can't ride a motorcycle"
Cyn starts the chant and I join in
Her rock let loose thuds against the chubby one's back
(Straw colored hair, fragile neck—the real thing—
still I look a whole lot like her, except I got a winter coat)
"white cracker, chew tobacco, can't ride a motorcycle—"
I feel sick, drop out

They show up at our school, the only white children
People whisper they're *trash*
The blond one named Dorothy is in my class
The teacher sits her next to me and I'm ashamed,
not just because of what we did, but side-by-side
the other kids will see how much we look alike
Before the standardized test begins, I lend her my extra pencil
She says thank you then looks on my paper
"Those are wrong," she whispers, pointing to the tiny boxes
I had marked with an X
I believe her even though I'm good at tests,
change my answers, get a low IQ that year
"What happened?" Mommy asks, eyes sad,
reading the scores sent home by the teacher
"Were you sick that day?"
"No, dumb."

Dog Dream 2

On the way to somewhere, I ignore the option of a waiting train
Bred for forced marches and dressed for winter,
I trudge alone, except for some unknowns
who drift through industrial dust and fog

A guard ahead signals trouble, his arms in mute chiasmus
Deconstruction at the border—for now, I can't go forward
The train sighs and a passenger appears:
my mother, risen from the dead, dressed in peach
and cradling a dog

I reach out and we exchange embraces
She then hands me the creature and she steps on board
Standing near the tracks, I watch her profile at the window,
craving her gaze

But her stare is fixed ahead and I remind myself she's dead
Yet, squirming in my arms, this thing with longish tail,
not quite domestic,
breathes in the locomotive's burning oil

Scribe

Morning in the house of ghosts,
bolt upright from dreams, detailing casualties

A word misspoke in mother's childhood
calls up the threat of rat for breakfast

The yellow gown in daughter's closet,
a drowning mermaid dripping dusty feet

I'm here to note a drizzle
the night of the car wreck

He missed the cake on account of a seizure

The sapphire band was cut

The pregnant bitch was sent to the pound

Abortion was never considered

Grandma called the preacher a monkey

The old man offered the little girl candy

The cousin started the touching,
so the whipping was for nothing

The tumor was big as a grapefruit and
the ladles and spoons were missing

Socks were not what he needed

That once on a country road
I was a fish in a parka
swimming toward lightning

Buttons

When my husband pours me coffee,
I smile the glassy lake
We won't speak of last night's scene,
fit of anguish, buttons flipping
How I tore my clothes

Premonition

Five a.m.: gown frayed at nipple, hair featherbed,
I softly tread the creaking floor,
shut the kitchen door to grind the beans,
and then reflected in the glass carafe,
see rings beneath my eyes

Now, with coffee cup in hand, I tip upon the dewy deck,
spy a creature crouching in the too-long grass
and its yellow stare and mean dumb face
make me stumble backwards—
Coyote in my yard

Then, safely back indoors:
my child comes down for breakfast
wearing fur—
 I crack the eggs; she eats
A day will come when she has grown a tail

Tale

In the tale of the donkey mask,
a girl's face was beneath, stitched in terror
Kicked and left for dead, yet she'd lived

A hoof print on her heart became
the key hole to a prison where she reeled her captor in
and bound him with her hair, stuffing his eyes
down her own gullet

Glutted, her own name became a choking stone
and the donkey's face became her own

They

They say he was aware
of having wasted his life
He'd been sober for three months
but then his cousin came to call,

kept after him to have a shot
He withstood the pressure for three days
before joining the binge,
a suicide of vodka and gin

Died the following week—
cracked his head, never woke up
I only know because they told me
They say his cousin was seen staggering

near the entrance of the hospital
Three years later, that man, too, was gone
His son and I have never discussed
what went down between our fathers
But we both know what they say

Poison

Love that little bottle
It takes me for a ride

Love that little bottle
A pleasant place to hide

Lovely little bottle
What a way to die

Behind a Blue Door

While moths seek their candles, I enter a hanging forest
I hear a cursing creek drown out a woman's hymn
On the path I sniff confusion, lavender and
the scent of rape
There's my mother, crouched on leaves,
mouthing to a crack of light
I encircle her
I die with her each night

Her Blood

Told you
not to bleed.
Didn't I
tell you, child,
not to bleed?

That iron
taint—he'll sniff.
He eyein'
you, child. Child,
hide your rags,

wash with lye,
eat river mud
and clay.
God, my child—
can't help her.

She got her
blood today.

The Sin of It

The summer I was twelve, I got beat
due to bloody pads found in my closet,
a private hoard of pride and shame

Neatly wrapped and stacked
along the shelf in place of shoes,
they bore witness to the juice

and ache of flowering
When my mother came into the room
with her sturdy broom

I was stretched out with a book
Hardly heard the closet creak
before she screamed "disgusting!"

She went at me with a strap
Made me gather up my trash—
I cried and railed at the injustice

What was the crime?
My blood was mine

Chain

A woman in a metal chair crochets a turquoise chain
A girl and younger boy sit on the stairs below her
The girl's toes stretch to touch a damp spot
on the cement walk
       The boy clutches his marble

A man appears at the gate and, in a jolly voice,
tells the children come for ice cream
The girl hops up
The woman stops crocheting
       But she says nothing

The girl steps over the garden hose, slips through the open gate
The man reaches for her skinny hand
Now they're waiting for the boy
 But he's kept his seat
       He won't go

Now the gate slams and the man mutters
       something under his breath
As they walk down the alley, the girl drags her feet,
even though the pavement's hot
She glances back—
       The boy is watching

Are people born a certain way?
One, brave enough to hold his own
Another, born to bend
Or are we simply stitched in moments?

The bathing suits are drying on the clothesline
The woman on the porch takes up her work

Raindrops

You said you'd walk between the raindrops
when you went into the hurricane, looking for the rest
So brave, I thought, peering through the blurry glass
In your Air Force jacket, no hat

I'd held onto a pole, afraid of being blown away
Being drenched was the least of it, we knew that
My wet haired, skinny dad,
charging out to save us

"sug"

I want to find the spot where you were standing
when you dropped this postcard into the box

I want to stand where you stood and see your view
Maybe if I walk this entire block on both sides

of the street and step where you stepped,
  I'll see a similar slant of sunlight

on the side of that red building
You stayed at a "Y," a picture on a postcard,
And now I'm here, holding it instead of you

I try to imagine you coming out of that doorway,
dwarfed by this city, with this very postcard
in your pocket, its letters printed neat enough

for me to read in the days you called me "*sug*"
Dad, I'm standing in front of a mailbox, crying
Dad, I'm trying to stand where you stood

Tikar Reunion

Daughter, you've come home weary, filled with self-doubt
You've sought me out to ask me how it happened:

I slept near the doorway
I was an early riser, so no one heard when I left
Each morning I rushed to the river
to compare my sister's catch with my own
One morning he was there and that was that

I didn't see his face, because my own was covered
I will tell you I felt the rip as you've imagined
Hissing bubbled from my core
When he carried me on board, I was a broken basket

So, when fruit slips through your hands,
don't blame yourself
Blame a morning breeze, a sunrise, a shrimp net

Dog Dream 3

There are knives scattered on the kitchen floor
Dog's been at it again, one of her pranks

Who would have guessed she would dare
put her paws upon the counter and lift the knives
from the sink with her teeth?

She'll be back
With a bleeding tongue

Hibiscus

you carried me in the crook
of your arm, my hand a fern
unfurling on your neck

threading through grass
toward the outhouse
you stopped to let me lean
into a flower taught me
a word
          hibiscus

One blazing Virginia afternoon

Sharon Dennis Wyeth grew up in Washington, D.C. A graduate of Anacostia High School, she received a B.A. with honors from Harvard University and an M.F.A. in Creative Writing, Memoir from Hunter College where she received the prestigious Shuster Award. Her poetry has appeared in *Cura Magazine, Squaw Valley Review, Drunken Boat, The Hollins Critic,* and *Cave Canem* anthologies. She is a member of the *Cave Canem* fellowship of African American poets. At the Community of Writers at Squaw Valley, she received the Lucille Clifton Fellowship. She has received additional fellowships from the Mid Atlantic Arts Foundation, the Virginia Center for Creative Arts and the Rockefeller Foundation. She has taught at Fordham and Hollins Universities and The New School. Ms. Wyeth is also an award-winning author of children's and young adult literature. *Black Eye,* the poet's first chapbook, was propelled by childhood memories. Ms. Wyeth has a background in music and theater. Her poetic voice is narrative, lyric and dramatic. Her writing explores themes of identity, trauma, domestic violence, resilience, and the intersection of cultural memory and the unconscious. She lives in Montclair, New Jersey with her husband, consultant, author and columnist Sims Wyeth.

www.ingramcontent.com/pod-product-compliance
Lightning Source LLC
LaVergne TN
LVHW051610080426
835510LV00020B/3223